T0063768

Plants
BITE
BACK

FIRST EDITION
Editor Sheila Hanly; **Art Editor** Jill Plank; **Senior Editor** Linda Esposito;
Senior Art Editor Diane Thistlethwaite; **US Editor** Regina Kahney; **Cover Designer** Margherita Gianni;
Production Melanie Dowland; **Picture Researcher** Andrea Sadler; **Illustrator** Peter Dennis;
Natural History Consultant Theresa Greenaway; **Reading Consultant** Linda Gambrell, PhD

THIS EDITION
Editorial Management by Oriel Square
Produced for DK by WonderLab Group LLC
Jennifer Emmett, Erica Green, Kate Hale, *Founders*

Editors Grace Hill Smith, Libby Romero, Michaela Weglinski;
Photography Editors Kelley Miller, Annette Kiesow, Nicole DiMella; **Managing Editor** Rachel Houghton;
Designers Project Design Company; **Researcher** Michelle Harris; **Copy Editor** Lori Merritt;
Indexer Connie Binder; **Proofreader** Larry Shea; **Reading Specialist** Dr. Jennifer Albro;
Curriculum Specialist Elaine Larson

Published in the United States by DK Publishing
1745 Broadway, 20th Floor, New York, NY 10019

Copyright © 2023 Dorling Kindersley Limited
DK, a Division of Penguin Random House LLC
22 23 24 25 26 10 9 8 7 6 5 4 3 2 1
001-333466-May/2023

A catalog record for this book
is available from the Library of Congress.
HC ISBN: 978-0-7440-6834-4
PB ISBN: 978-0-7440-6835-1

DK books are available at special discounts when purchased in bulk for sales promotions, premiums,
fundraising, or educational use. For details, contact: DK Publishing Special Markets,
1745 Broadway, 20th Floor, New York, NY 10019
SpecialSales@dk.com

Printed and bound in China

The publisher would like to thank the following for their kind permission to reproduce their images:
a=above; c=center; b=below; l=left; r=right; t=top; b/g=background

123RF.com: Ruttawee Jaigunta 7bl, Feng Yu 14tl; **Alamy Stock Photo:** Nick Greaves 41tr, Jurgen Freund / Nature Picture Library 30b,
Ariadne Van Zandbergen 7c, 37l; **Dreamstime.com:** EPhotocorp 21tr, Guinevra 10cla, Esben Hansen 9cra, Jessicahyde 25br,
Kasto80 30cl, Craig Russell 11cra, Aleksandr Makarenko 29tr; **Getty Images:** Thomas Roche 6clb, 39b, Ted Mead / Stone 7cb, 31;
naturepl.com: Kim Taylor 13; **Science Photo Library:** George Bernard 14cr, Hermann Eisenbeiss 14br;
Shutterstock.com: John Ceulemans 23cra, E-lona 4-5, Alex Farias 30tl, Nick Greaves 6bl, 40-41, GrigoryL 32b,
Luka Hercigonja 12b, JoannaTkaczuk 45b, kelifamily 45tl, Dr. Norbert Lange 19tr, Michael Moloney 26b,
Sakda Narathipwan 12cla, pisitpong2017 45tr, Rainbow_dazzle 35cr, Usanee 18clb

Cover images: *Front:* **Dreamstime.com:** Karin De Mamiel, Verastuchelova bc, br;
Back: **Shutterstock.com:** BeataGFX clb, Kazakova Maryia cra, shockfactor.de cla

All other images © Dorling Kindersley
For more information see: www.dkimages.com

For the curious
www.dk.com

Plants
BITE
BACK

Richard Platt

CONTENTS

PLANT POWER

Plants cover the surface of Earth. Without them, we could not survive. One of their most important things plants do is to provide food for animals and people.

But not all plants can be munched for lunch. Some make bitter poisons to keep animals from eating them.

There are no flies on this plant—it's eaten them all! See how the Venus flytrap catches insects on pages 8–11.

NORTH AMERICA

EUROPE

AFRICA

Beware of the giant saguaro cactus on page 39—it's covered in thousands of sharp spines.

SOUTH AMERICA

Find out why this tree is called the candelabra tree on page 40.

Some arm themselves with spikes or stings. Others turn the tables completely—they catch animals and eat THEM!

Every country in the world has its share of stinging, scratching, and biting plants. This map shows where some of them grow—and where you will find them in the pages ahead.

Self Defense
Plants can't run away like animals can. Poisons, thorns, and other adaptations are how plants defend themselves against threats.

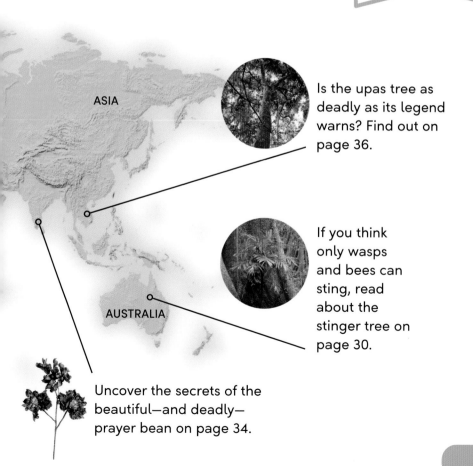

ASIA

Is the upas tree as deadly as its legend warns? Find out on page 36.

If you think only wasps and bees can sting, read about the stinger tree on page 30.

AUSTRALIA

Uncover the secrets of the beautiful—and deadly—prayer bean on page 34.

GREEDY GREEN GUZZLERS

On the edge of a swamp, a damselfly flies over a plant with strange-looking leaves. The damselfly hovers, then lands. SNAP! The comb-shaped sides of the leaf spring together and trap the damselfly.

The plant is a Venus flytrap. It is a carnivorous, or meat-eating, plant. These plants are unusual. Of the 435,000 different kinds of plants on Earth's surface, more than 600 are carnivorous.

Carnivorous plants grow in marshes or bogs. Boggy soil does not contain enough of the minerals that plants need to grow well. Carnivorous plants get an extra supply of these minerals by eating insects. They can survive without eating insects, but the extra minerals help them to grow better.

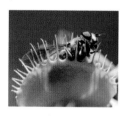

The Venus flytrap grows in marshland in North and South Carolina.

Catching insects is not easy when you are a plant. The Venus flytrap has no eyes to see flies. It has no ears to hear the hum of a honeybee. So how does it lure its lunch?

Like every trap, the Venus flytrap contains bait. Sugary nectar covers the leaves. Insects smell the nectar. They think it's mealtime. They are right, but they never guess THEY are on the menu.

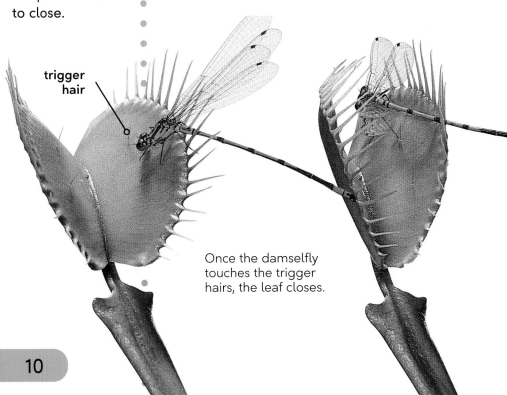

trigger hair

Once the damselfly touches the trigger hairs, the leaf closes.

Three tiny hairs on each leaf act as triggers. As soon as an insect touches the hairs, **TWANG** goes the trap. In less than a second, the sides of the leaf close in over the insect.

After 30 minutes, the trap has shut tightly and filled with liquid. Over a week or two, most of the insect's body dissolves into dead-insect soup. The plant absorbs this liquid food through its leaf surface.

Saving Energy
To conserve energy, the Venus flytrap only closes if the trigger hairs are touched multiple times.

Expiration Date
After catching three to four insects, a Venus flytrap's leaves die. The plant grows new leaves to replace them.

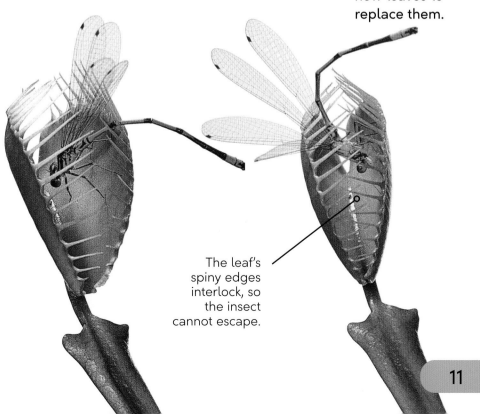

The leaf's spiny edges interlock, so the insect cannot escape.

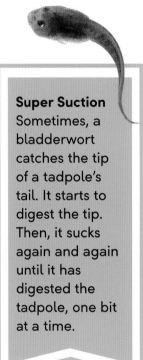

The Venus flytrap is the only plant with deadly jaws. The bladderwort, another meat-eating plant, has a sneakier way of catching lunch. It sucks up its victims like a vacuum cleaner!

A bladderwort eats tiny water insects and fish. It can swallow fry, or baby fish, in a single bite.

Super Suction Sometimes, a bladderwort catches the tip of a tadpole's tail. It starts to digest the tip. Then, it sucks again and again until it has digested the tadpole, one bit at a time.

Bladderwort stems and flowers grow above water.

Bladderworts are among the most common of carnivorous plants. They float in ponds. They grow in very wet ground. They even live in puddles of rainwater that form in the cup-shaped leaves of some plants.

Snappy Bloom
A bladderwort's flower looks like a yellow snapdragon.

This mosquito larva is too big for the bladderwort to swallow—so the larva will probably wiggle free.

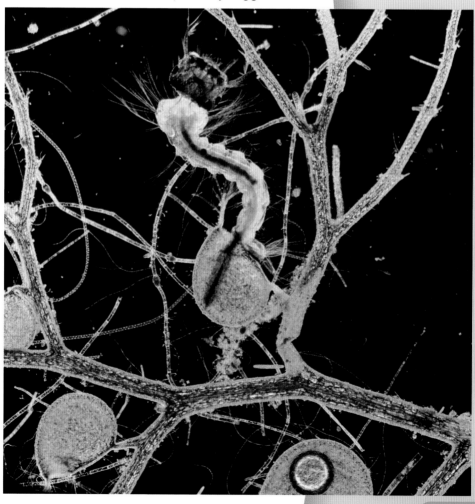

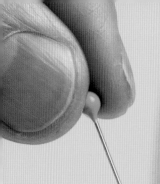

Tiny Trap
A bladderwort's trap is about the size of a pinhead.

Plants That Eat People!
Carnivorous plants mostly eat insects. People-eating plants, such as this one from the movie *Little Shop of Horrors*, exist only in science fiction.

You would need a microscope to see a bladderwort catch its prey. On each of its roots are a number of traps that look like tiny bubbles. Each trap has a little door that shuts tight. To set the trap, the plant sucks water out of it. This makes the trap's springy wall cave inward. There are tiny trigger hairs on the trap. If an insect, such as a water flea, touches the hairs, the trap door suddenly opens.

A water flea gets too close to a bladderwort.

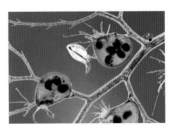

The bladderwort digests its meal.

The sucked-in sides of the trap spring out. Water rushes in, sucking the flea with it. **SNAP!** The door closes again, trapping the insect inside. This happens in one-fiftieth of a second—faster than the eye can see.

Then, a mixture of chemicals in the trap slowly dissolves the water flea's body.

Fatal Attraction
Bladderworts can't chase prey, so they lure it in instead. The plant releases an irresistibly sweet smell. When the prey comes in to investigate, the bladderwort traps it.

Unlike bladderworts, pitcher plants have no moving parts. Instead, they drown their prey in pools of liquid. These pools are a mixture of water and digestive juices. They form in the plant's leaves, which are shaped like pitchers.

The largest pitcher plants grow in Borneo, an island in Southeast Asia. These giant pitchers are big enough to trap insects, small birds, frogs, and even rats! The monkey cup pitcher plant gets its name because thirsty monkeys drink from its pitchers. Humans use the pitchers, too— as buckets and sometimes as cooking pots.

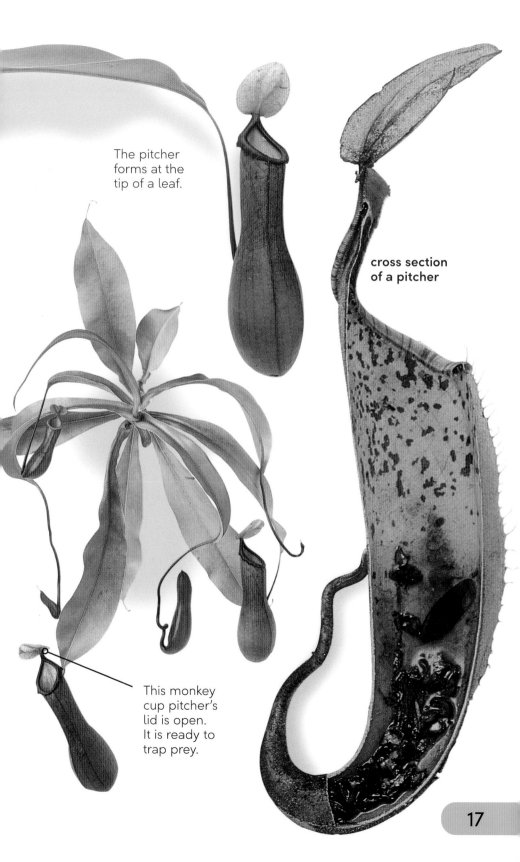

The pitcher forms at the tip of a leaf.

cross section of a pitcher

This monkey cup pitcher's lid is open. It is ready to trap prey.

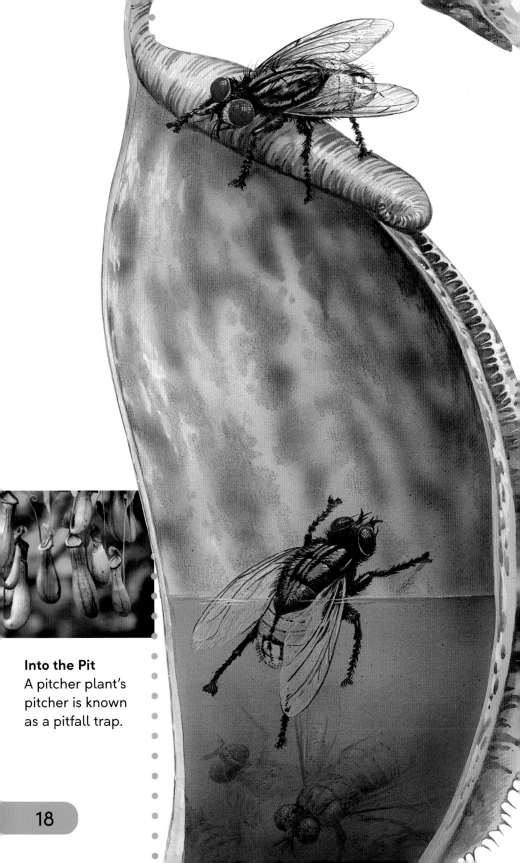

Into the Pit
A pitcher plant's pitcher is known as a pitfall trap.

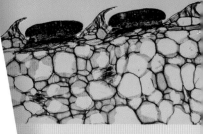

But how does a pitcher plant catch its prey? Imagine a fly buzzing through the jungle. It spots a brightly colored pitcher. The fly lands on the pitcher's slippery edge. It smells nectar around the rim. It sees shiny ridges leading down into the pitcher. The hungry fly climbs into the pitcher to suck up the nectar.

But the inner surface of the pitcher is covered in loose, waxy flakes. The fly begins to slip and slide. As it scrabbles and struggles, the waxy flakes peel away and the fly loses its grip. **SPLASH!** It sinks into the liquid and drowns, and the pitcher plant begins to digest its latest meal.

Dissolving Prey
Glands on the inner surface of the pitcher make digestive juices that dissolve the plant's prey.

Cobra Lily
The cobra lily is a pitcher plant that grows in northern California and southern Oregon in the United States. Its long, curved pitcher flares out at the top, making it look like a striking cobra. Forked red leaves coming out of the pitcher's mouth look like fangs or a snake's tongue.

Sundew plants are nature's own flypaper. Every leaf of the sundew plant is covered in fine, sticky hairs. Each hair has a glue-like droplet at its tip that gives the plant its name: in sunlight, they sparkle like dew.

The droplets are glands that produce nectar to lure insects.

The Next Generation
Some sundew species self-pollinate when they close their flowers. Others produce seeds.

Although sundews are found all over the world, the greatest variety grows in Australia. The smallest is no bigger than a shirt button. But a few types grow into sticky bushes higher than a grown-up's waist.

Deadly Combination Assassin bugs aren't affected by a sundew's goo. They hide on the plant, waiting to catch other insects.

A group of sundew plants growing in poor, boggy soil

Why Buy Flypaper?
Instead of using flypaper, people in countries such as Portugal sometimes hang up bunches of sundew plants to catch flies.

When an insect lands on a sundew's leaf, just one touch of one hair is enough to catch and hold the insect.

When the insect tries to get free, it touches another hair... then another.

A fly gets quickly stuck.

As it struggles, more hairs bend toward it. Their sticky tips clamp the wiggling creature tightly. The more the insect struggles, the tighter the leaf grips. Eventually, the insect's body is crushed and it dies a sticky death.

The Final Battle
Sundews don't poison their prey. Insects either suffocate in the sticky goo or die of exhaustion from trying to escape.

Long Meal
It can take a sundew about 15 minutes to kill an insect. But it can take several weeks for the plant to digest its meal.

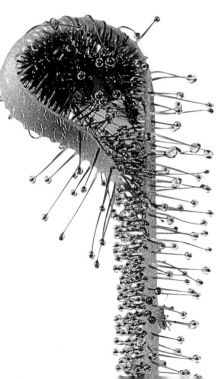

The leaf pours out digestive juices to dissolve the fly's body.

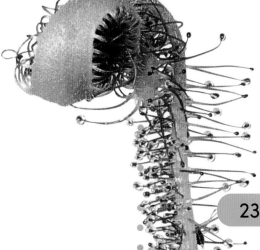

23

DEADLY WEEDS

Key to Plant Symbols

⚡ stinging

😖 poisonous

☠ deadly poisonous

Carnivorous plants are no danger to humans, but some other plants are. If you took a walk in this North American woodland, would you spot the plants you should avoid?

Some plants make mild poisons to stop animals from eating them.

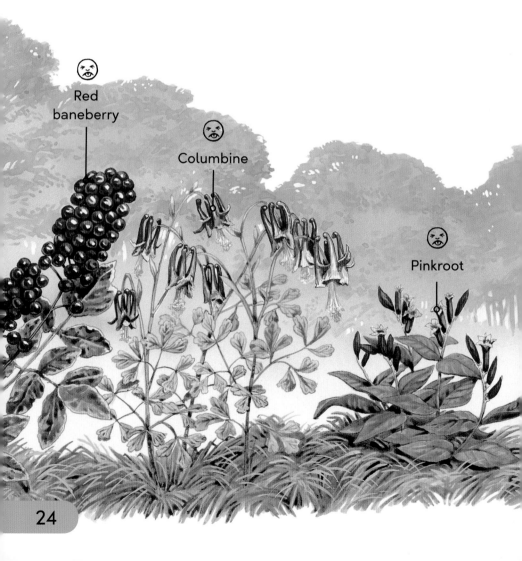

😖 Red baneberry

😖 Columbine

😖 Pinkroot

If you touched or ate one, it would sting you or make you sick. Some plants even make poisons that can kill.

So never touch or bite a strange plant. It might bite back!

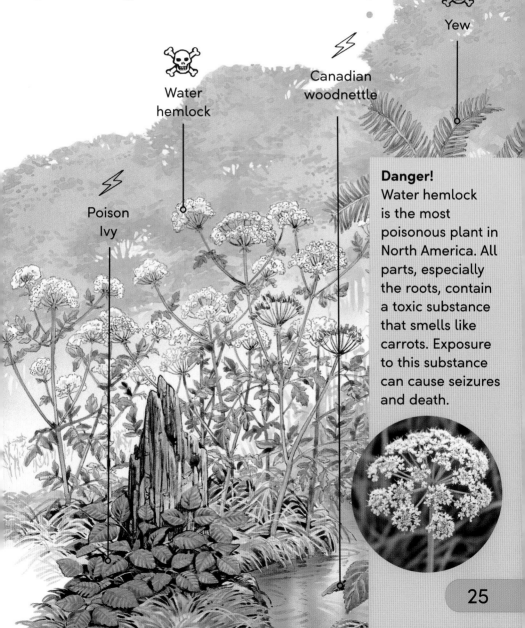

Yew

Canadian woodnettle

Water hemlock

Poison Ivy

Danger!
Water hemlock is the most poisonous plant in North America. All parts, especially the roots, contain a toxic substance that smells like carrots. Exposure to this substance can cause seizures and death.

Stinging plants use chemicals to keep animals from eating them.

Poison ivy is a stinging plant that grows all over North America. The plant contains a sticky oil. If you brush against the plant, the oil that oozes out from bruised leaves or stems can spread onto your skin.

Some people feel a sting immediately. Others feel nothing at first, but hours later, their skin starts to blister and itch unbearably. In a few days, the blisters turn into oozing, crusted sores.

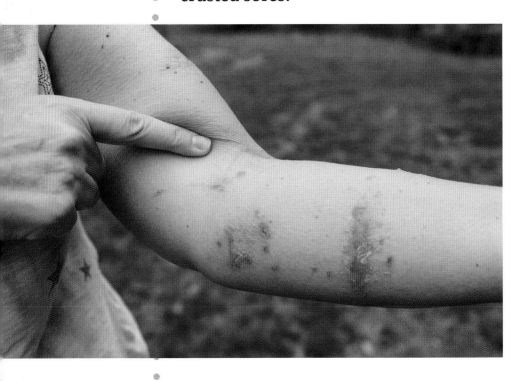

three leaflets
of a poison
ivy plant

Leave It Alone!
"Leaves of three, let it be." For ages, people have remembered this saying to avoid poison ivy. Poison ivy isn't always easy to spot. But it does have three leaflets attached to a single stem.

You can develop these sores without ever touching a poison ivy plant. Its oil can be spread by pets, garden tools, and sports equipment— in fact, anything that touches a bruised or broken plant.

Some stinging plants have weak chemicals, but they can still pack a painful punch. To do this, they need to get their poisons right through the skin.

The stinging nettle does this with millions of tiny, hollow spikes. If you touch a stinging nettle leaf, the spikes will prick your skin. The tips of the spikes break off and release acid from the plant. The acid flows through the hollow spikes and into your skin.

Dock to the Rescue
The dock plant, which often grows near nettles, can ease the pain of a nettle rash if its leaves are crushed and pressed onto the sting.

The tiny, glass-like tip snaps off when the spike is touched.

The spike is filled with chemicals from base to tip.

Once the tip has broken off, the remaining point is sharp enough to pierce skin.

The acid causes a burning, itching rash with red, raised bumps. Fortunately, this usually goes away after an hour or two, although some people suffer for up to 24 hours.

Tall Plant
Stinging nettles grow in groups. Full-grown plants can be more than 10 feet (3 m) tall.

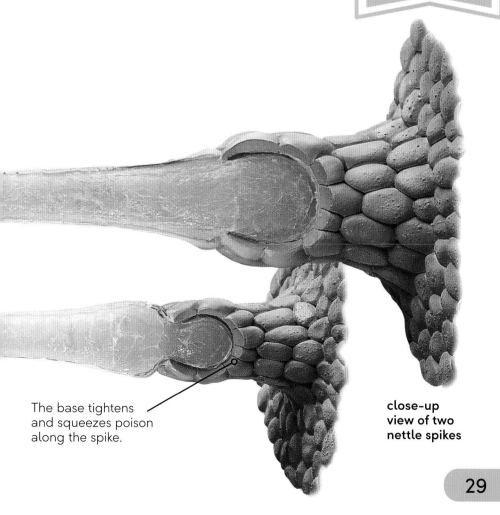

The base tightens and squeezes poison along the spike.

close-up view of two nettle spikes

Venomous Tree
Scientists have discovered that Australia's stinging trees contain a neurotoxin. It's similar to the venom found in spiders and cone snails.

Silver Lining?
Researchers are studying the stinging tree's toxins. What they learn could help them develop newer, better pain medicines.

Nettles are not very harmful to humans, but they have a highly dangerous relative—the stinger tree of Australia. Its name alone should warn you of danger.

Stinger tree leaves are covered in hollow hairs with very sharp tips. The hairs work like the needle of a doctor's syringe. If you touch a leaf, the hair tips break off and the hairs inject poison into your skin.

If you brush your arm against a stinger tree, it will give you a sting you will never forget. Your arm will throb painfully all day. It will still tingle two weeks later. But if you happened to get stung all over by stinger tree leaves, the pain would be so bad you would not be able to walk or get up. You could even receive enough poison to kill you.

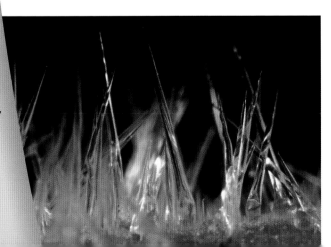

Wolf Killer
Another name for the monkshood plant is wolfsbane. It got this name because its roots were once used to poison wolves.

Many dangerous plants have no sting. Some are even quite beautiful. You would never guess from its pretty blue or purple flowers that monkshood contains a powerful poison. Its name is aconitine and even tiny amounts of it can kill.

The poison, which is found in all parts of the plant, was once used on the tips of spears and arrows for hunting and battle.

Purple Poison
People often grow monkshood because it has such pretty flowers. But beware of this plant. Swallowing any part of it could have fatal consequences.

**close-up of a
monkshood
flower**

The roots, leaves,
stems, and even
the flowers of the
monkshood
are poisonous.

Weighing Them Up
Because prayer bean seeds are all nearly exactly the same weight and size, they were once used as weights to weigh gold and diamonds.

Like the monkshood, the bright red seeds of the prayer bean plant look harmless. People in India used the seeds to make necklaces.

But wearing a prayer bean necklace is a bad idea. Each little seed contains enough poison to kill a grown-up. If the tough

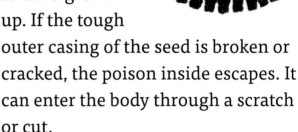

outer casing of the seed is broken or cracked, the poison inside escapes. It can enter the body through a scratch or cut.

prayer bean plant

For the Birds
Prayer bean seeds are toxic to humans and can harm cats, dogs, and horses—but not birds. Birds eat and spread their seeds.

Crab's Eyes
Prayer bean seeds are two-thirds scarlet and one-third black. One of their common names is crab's eyes.

Tall Tale

In 1783, *London Magazine* published an article in which a Dutch traveler told about his encounters with the upas tree. He claimed that just breathing in its vapors could be deadly. The author made it all up. The Dutch traveler wasn't even a real person. It didn't matter. The legend of the deadly upas tree was born and flourished.

Toxic Name

"Upus" comes from the Malay word for poison.

Hundreds of years ago, tales of the deadly upas tree became legend. Found in Southeast Asia and Australia, the "tree of poisons" was reportedly powerful enough to kill birds that flew over it, and anyone who slept in its shade would never wake up.

These descriptions are not true: birds perch unharmed in the tree's branches, and sleeping under the tree is perfectly safe.

But the tales are based in truth. The sap of the tree contains a deadly poison. A scratch from the bark causes a painful rash. Poison taken from the sap can stop the heart from beating in just a few minutes.

Deadly Darts
Indigenous people in South America used ingredients from trees there to make one of the world's most powerful natural poisons: curare. They spread the poison on darts, which they shot from long bamboo blowpipes to hunt animals.

solid curare

bottle of curare

darts tipped with curare

dart case

NATURE'S DAGGERS

Many plants, such as brambles, protect themselves with thorns and spines instead of poison. Prickly plants sprout almost everywhere.

Bramble

In the deserts of America grow the spiniest of all plants—the cactus family. Cacti (plural for "cactus") have spines instead of leaves. These sharp spines keep thirsty animals from munching the cactus's juicy stem. The spines also help the cactus to get water. Mist and dew collect on the spines and drip or trickle down to water the cactus's roots.

Going Fishing?
In the past, people have used the strong, hooked spines of the "barrel" cactus as fishing hooks.

The fluffy stems look like rabbits' ears.

Mexican "hedgehog" cactus

Cactus spines are bad enough, but the tufts of stiff, fine hair that grow on some cacti can also cause terrible pain. Each hair has a hook on the end. Once stuck in your flesh, the hairs are almost impossible to remove.

Many people have innocent-looking "bunny ears" cacti in their homes. They are part of the prickly pear family and have hundreds of hairs on each of their pads (flattened stems).

Saguaro Cactus
Cactus plants can get very tall. The biggest is the saguaro cactus. In 150 years, it can grow as tall as a five-story building.

Look Out!
Candelabra tree stems contain milky sap that can burn your skin and even cause blindness if it gets in your eyes.

Poinsettia

Spurge plants are fleshy, bushy shrubs with colorful leaves and flowers. The popular poinsettia plant is a member of the spurge family.

Many wild spurges are spiny as well as colorful. The sharpest, spikiest spurge of all is the candelabra tree.

The candelabra tree gets its name from its unusual shape. It looks like a candelabra, or candle stand.

A candelabra tree growing on the African plains

However, candelabra trees are not small. They are huge. In South Africa, where they grow wild, candelabra trees may reach the height of a house.

Butterflies and bees visit the clusters of tiny, yellow flowers that bloom from fall to winter, which helps pollinate these trees. Some birds also nest in the candelabra's branches and eat seeds from the tree's fruit.

Tipped with Fire
The candelabra tree's yellow flowers grow at the tips of its branches. So not only is the tree shaped like a candle stand, but from a distance it looks like the candles in the stand are glowing!

TAMING THE PLANTS

Plants that bite back are not bad plants. They are just plants that have smart ways of surviving in a tough world. And while we humans may curse their prickles and stings, we have also learned how useful they can be.

Cattle herders in some parts of Africa build thorny fences to keep their animals safe. In Mexico, hedges of prickly pear cacti protect some homes.

Even stinging plants have had their uses to humans.

In chilly weather, ancient Roman soldiers warmed their legs by beating them with nettle plants.

Women once used plants instead of makeup. They rubbed their cheeks with the woolly leaves of mullein plants. Mullein leaves are covered in soft, fine hairs. These hairs irritated the women's skin and gave their cheeks a bright, rosy glow.

mullein plant

But what use is a poisonous plant? The answer may surprise you. Plant poisons that kill in large doses can heal in smaller amounts.

Doctors once used aconitine, from the deadly monkshood plant, to help calm patients' nerves.

You could die from heart failure if you ate just four leaves from the foxglove plant. But foxglove poison is now used to treat some heart disorders.

Nature's Apothecary
Many plants have developed chemical defenses to protect themselves. Understanding how those substances interact with the human body is the key to finding future cures.

foxglove

And today, scientists are extracting anti-cancer drugs from the poisonous yew tree and the toxic rosy periwinkle shrub.

Who knows what uses will be found for deadly plants in the future?

yew

rosy periwinkle

yew tree

GLOSSARY

Absorb
To soak up or take in something

Acid
A burning chemical

Aconitine
(ah-CON-eh-teen)
A deadly poison found in the
monkshood plant

Bait
Something that encourages prey
to come closer to a trap

Cactus
A family of North American plants
with fleshy stems used to store
water

Carnivorous
(car-NIV-er-uss)
A meat eater. A carnivorous plant
gets extra minerals from the dead
bodies of animals.

Curare
An arrow poison made from
a mixture of plants

Desert
Land where little or no rain falls

Digestive juices
Liquid filled with chemicals that
help to break down food so that
it can be absorbed by a plant
or animal

Fry
Baby fish

Glands
Structures inside a plant or animal
that produce chemicals such as
digestive juices

Larva
A young animal that is completely
different from an adult animal of
the same kind. For example, a
caterpillar is the larva of a butterfly.

Minerals
Inorganic (neither plant nor animal)
substances that all living things
need in order to grow

Nectar
A liquid made by flowering plants

Poison
A substance that kills or damages
living things

Prey
Animals that are caught and eaten
by plants or other animals

Root
The part of a plant that takes in
water and minerals

Trigger hairs
Sensitive hairs that grow on plants
near their traps. If touched, the
hairs send a message to the plant
to make it shut its trap.

INDEX

QUIZ

Answer the questions to see what you have learned. Check your answers in the key below.

1. Where do carnivorous plants grow?

2. How does a Venus flytrap lure insects?

3. What carnivorous plants suck up their prey like a vacuum cleaner?

4. What kind of plant works like flypaper?

5. What are a stinger tree's leaves covered in?

6. What kind of prickly plants grow in American deserts?

7. Name two kinds of spurge plants.

8. True or False: Plant poisons can be used to treat disease.

1. Marshes or bogs 2. With nectar 3. Bladderworts 4. Sundews
5. Hollow hairs with sharp tips 6. Cacti 7. Poinsettia and candelabra
tree 8. True